Seamus

The Patron Snake of Ireland

(a wee bit of nonsense)

written & illustrated by Sharon R. Takerer

Grania

JET   JFA

Thanks for believing!

ISBN 1-893757-28-5

10 9 8 7 6 5 4 3 2 1
Printed in Mexico

Published by E.T. NEDDER Publishing. No part of this book may be reprinted or transmitted in any form or by any means, electronic or mechanical, or by an information retrieval system without permission in writing from the publisher.

Additional copies of this publication may be purchased by sending check or money order for $9.95 plus $4.00 postage and handling for #28-8 : E.T. NEDDER Publishing, PMB #299, 9121 East Tanque Verde, STE #105, Tucson, Arizona 85749-8390. Or call toll free 1-877-817-2742.   Fax: 1-520-760-5883   www.NEDDERPublishing.com

Long, long ago in Emerald Isle there lived a darling fellow by the name of Seamus (Shā-mus) O'Slither.

Seamus lived in the driest nook of Berrigan's Bog along with his sisters Faith and Begorrah, and grandmother Maggie. They lived their lives in great privacy, due to the fact there were few others of their kind in the land.

Grandma Maggie took great care of the little snaklings telling them tales of their ancestry and how their Mum and Dad slipped aboard a Viking ship to seek a better life for their family.

Grandma Maggie offered to watch over Seamus and his sss-isters who were no more than three little eggs at the time of their parent's departure. Although much time had passed, they waited faithfully for their return.

3

The little serpents favored stories of their kin like "Anxious" Angus MacSlither a grand plaid snake from Scotland, and the fearsome tales of a

4

man named Patrick who supposedly drove the snakes away from the beautiful land of Ireland.

"Perhaps", Maggie sighed, "that is why Mr. & Mrs. O'Slither were so long in returning".

Grandma Maggie's stories were always the best part of the day for Seamus and his sss-isters,

5

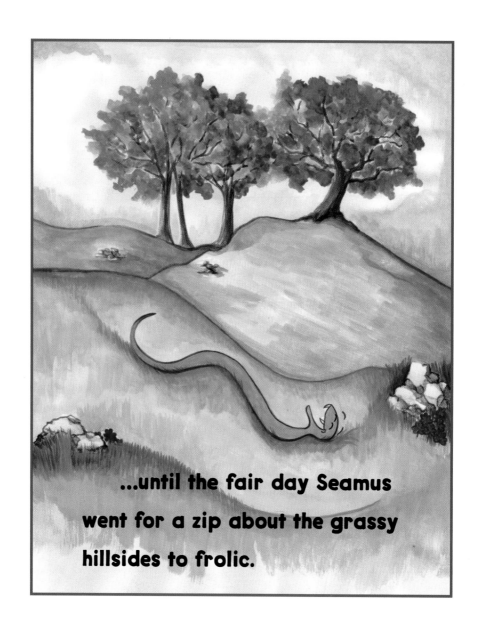

...until the fair day Seamus went for a zip about the grassy hillsides to frolic.

Knowing that he ought to be careful when and where he chose to frolic, the glorious breezes and dancing trees caught Seamus up in merriment, and he slipped and zipped down the hill in a fit of fun until he heard the strong ringing voice of a man!

Startled, Seamus curled around a rock to listen to the stories this stranger had to tell.

When Seamus peeked between two blades of grass, he gasped in a shakey, snakey way. There were numbers of people sitting about listening to this man, all enchanted by his words,

8

spellbound like he and his sss-isters became when Grandma Maggie told her tales! Seamus just had to listen to what sort of stories people liked to hear.

Everyday after his breakfast chores were done, Seamus slid away to the hillside and hid behind the rocks and clumps of clover to hear the man speak again. This God must be wonderful, Seamus thought, and he found himself wondering what God looked like.

Seamus was charmed by the expressions of the man, and he particularly liked the story of the great Creator who fashioned all the earth and it's subjects.

This very passionate story-teller told all of the eager listeners that the Creator–God, loved every creature great and small.

Seamus hissed a happy hiss, and tried to imagine the goodness of God loving even the strangest of creatures like himself.

Lost in his thoughts Seamus was shaken when suddenly the man reached over toward Seamus' secret spot and snatched a clover to use in his story.

Suddenly Seamus darted out in a streak
sending all of the Colleens scattering and
shrieking prayers to the creator for protection!

Seamus in a panic started for home as fast
as his little snakey ribs could transport him,
when . . .

EEEEK!

PATRICK!

—terror of terrors—a large firm hand reached down to stop him!

EEEEEEK! Patrick! Don't be playin' with the likes of him!" shouted a few of the people who remained.

"Be at peace," assured Patrick.

PATRICK!?! Seamus panicked...will he crush me or send me sailin' through the air like a spear? Seamus pinched his tiny snake eyes shut in fear. Seamus O'Slither had come face-to-face with the great St. Patrick whose reputation for driving snakes away was legendary!

15

As moments passed, Seamus popped
one eye open to figure out what to expect
next. "Please don't chase me into the sea!"
cried Seamus.

A softened smile appeared and the
furry eyebrows on Patrick's face raised in
amusement. "Fear not, little creature",
said Patrick.

"I am most pleased to meet you! You are the handiwork of the Lord that we haven't often seen in this land!

"Seamus' eyes grew wide and his tiny thumping serpent heart began to ease.

"What brings you to our gathering, wee one?"

"'Tis the stories you tell!" whispered Seamus. "I come everyday and coil midst the rocks and clovers just to hear you!"

18

"You are most welcome to come to our gathering every day," said Patrick. At these words, a new friendship was born.

The very next morning, Patrick introduced Seamus to the people who gathered regularly to hear the lessons of their special storyteller. As the days followed, Seamus often enjoyed more personal chats with the great saint.

"Tell me Seamus," Patrick said one day, "Why are you such a shy creature?"

Seamus' normal complexion brought on a blush, and he confessed to Patrick the tales of his kind being chased from the land and the close calls Grandmother Maggie had with the Kilgarry snake stomping brigade.

"Snake stomping brigade?" puzzled Patrick, "I've never heard of such a thing!"

"Oh, yes!" insisted Seamus, "They call
themselves step dancers who aim to stomp
the life out of wee snaklets like meself."

21

"Why Seamus," said Patrick, "'tis no wonder you have such a low estimation of yourself! Certainly, this is not true!"

"Dear Patrick," whispered Seamus, "estimation of one's self can't get much lower than that of a snake, now can it?" Seamus smiled revealing his gentle humor.

"I would indeed be honored if you would become my assistant," announced Patrick and Seamus felt another frenzy of merriment about to take place.

"Thank you, good sir," responded Seamus, "a true honor to be sure!"

The very next day Seamus brought Grandma Maggie to meet his mentor. Grandma Maggie was quite proud of Seamus who helped Patrick teach the sign of the cross to the Irish children with the assistance of his sisters Faith and Begorrah.

Soon, Seamus and his little family
endeared themselves to the following
of St. Patrick.

As time passed Seamus discovered
a talent for art, and began creating
decorative patterns for Patrick's mantles
and book coverings. Seamus simply would
express his joy and merriment by slipping,
slithering, and frolicking in the
shapes of knots and curls collecting
the green juice of the grass and
transferring the patterns to cloth.

St. Patrick was so impressed he sent the designs to nearby monasteries where they would eventually be used to decorate the book of Kells.

One of Patrick's most famous lessons bears the influence of Seamus' faithfulness even to this day!

As Patrick's apprentice, Seamus would fetch the clover needed for Patrick's sermon on the Trinity.

From that time, Patrick's people would forever call the local clovers "Seamrocks" (Shamrocks) meaning "flowers from the hiding place of Seamus."

With the passage of many years, Seamus followed Patrick all about the land teaching the villages about the love of God.

And though 'twas told that Seamus eventually met a she-snake ("Sharon of Erin") upon a visit to the North, he and Patrick remained friends to the end.

Seamus and Sharon fell in love, married, and raised a fine son by the name of Slattery and that is yet another snake's tail!

The END

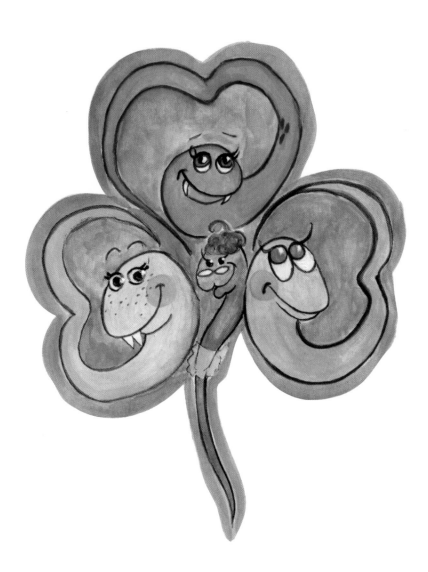